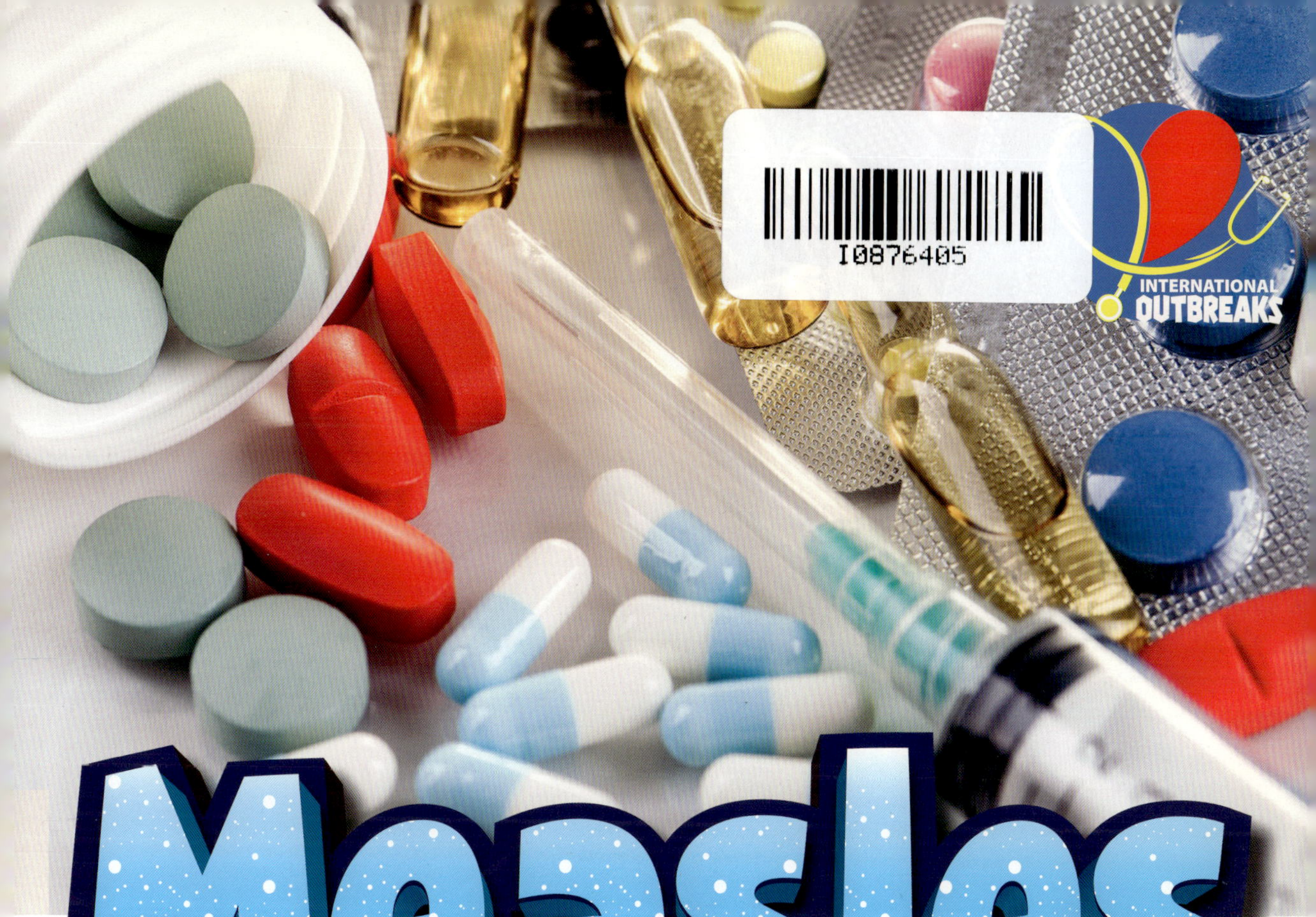

INTERNATIONAL OUTBREAKS

Measles

Heather C. Hudak

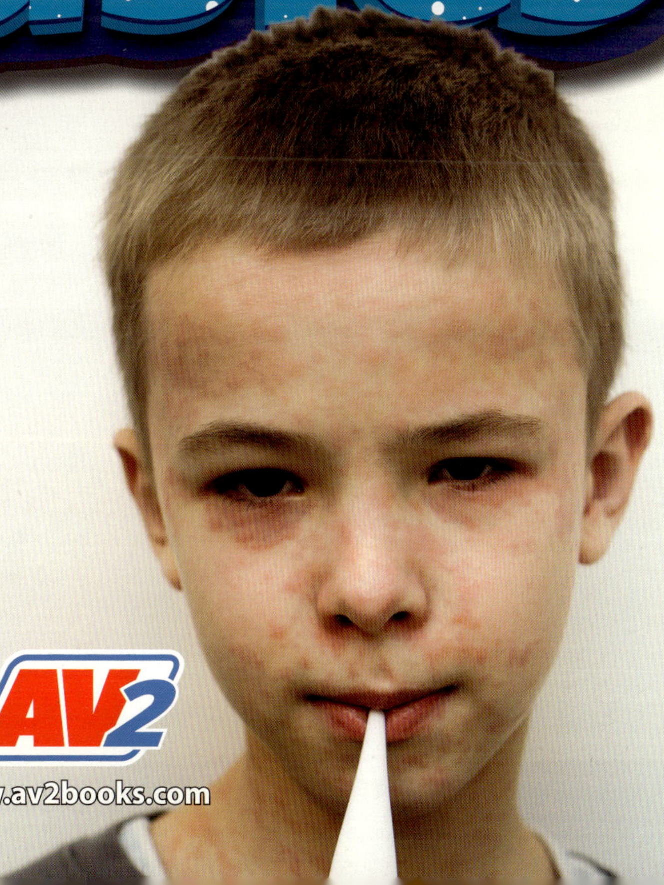

AV2
www.av2books.com

Step 1
Go to **www.av2books.com**

Step 2
Enter this unique code
YUVMTS76W

Step 3
Explore your interactive eBook!

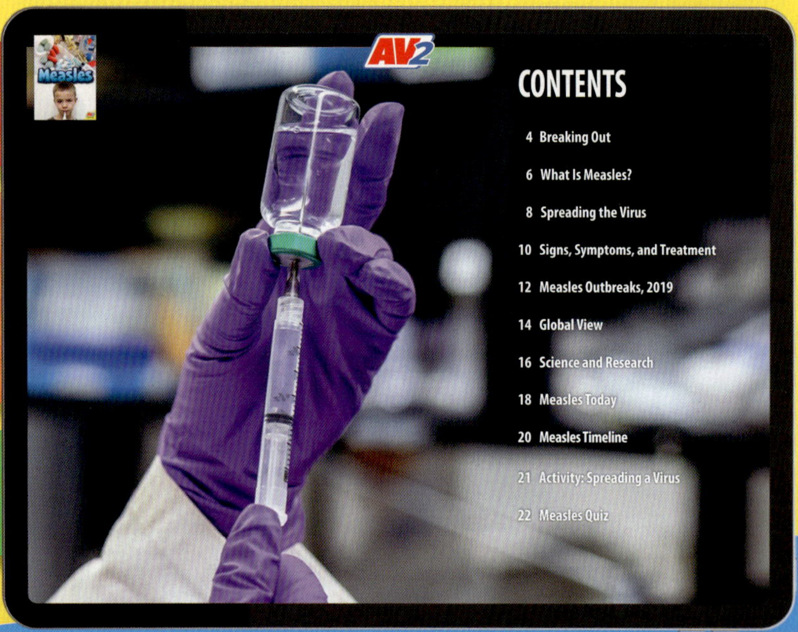

AV2 is optimized for use on any device

Your interactive eBook comes with...

Contents
Browse a live contents page to easily navigate through resources

Audio
Listen to sections of the book read aloud

Videos
Watch informative video clips

Weblinks
Gain additional information for research

Try This!
Complete activities and hands-on experiments

Key Words
Study vocabulary, and complete a matching word activity

Quizzes
Test your knowledge

Slideshows
View images and captions

... and much, much more!

INTERNATIONAL OUTBREAKS

Measles

CONTENTS

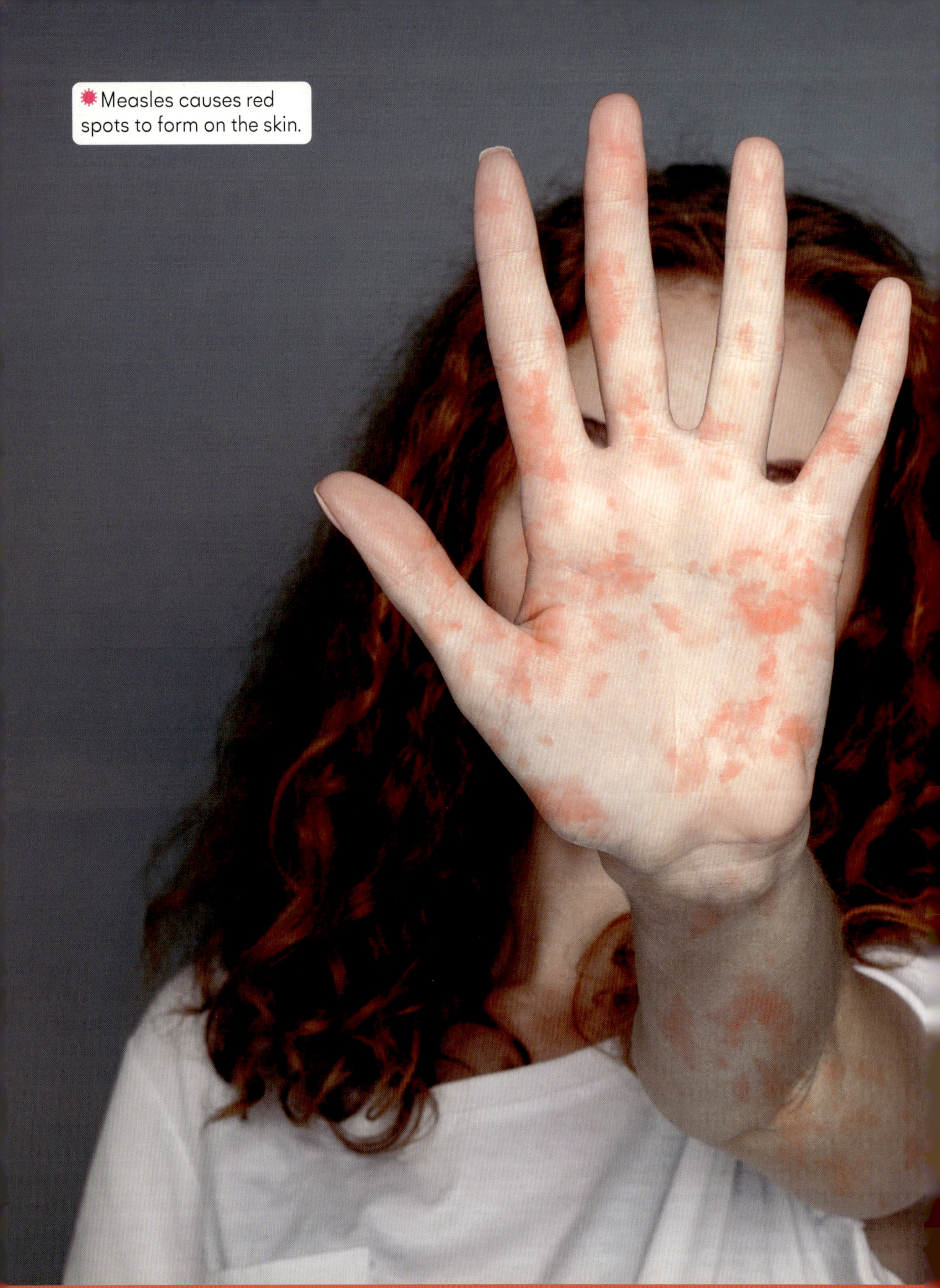

Measles causes red spots to form on the skin.

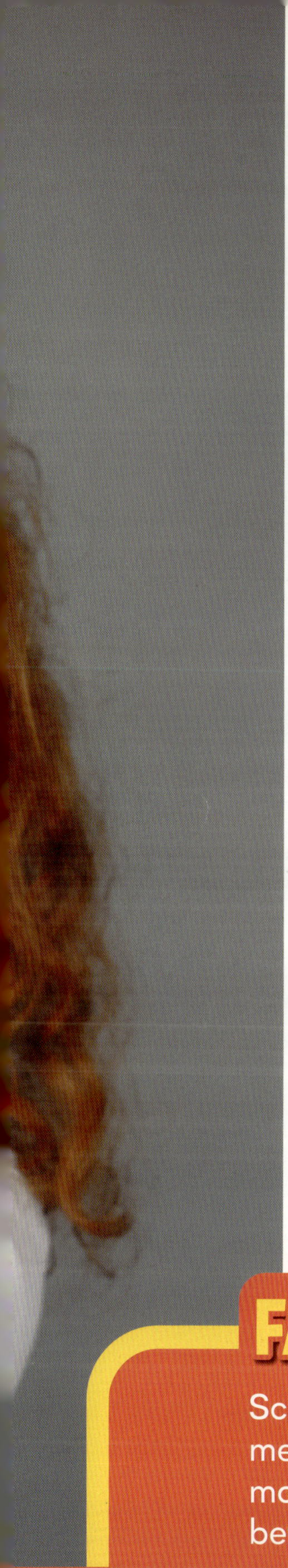

Breaking Out

Viruses are tiny germs. They are found in all kinds of environments. Viruses **infect** living beings. Hundreds of viruses are known to infect humans. Scientists track how many people are infected by viruses each year. They also take note of when and where **diseases** caused by viruses show up. Scientists look at how many cases happen at a certain time and place. Then, they look at the number of cases in that place in past years. This helps them find out how many cases are normal for that particular time and place each year.

Sometimes, there are more cases of a virus than normal. This is called an outbreak. It can last days, months, or years. Some viruses spread very quickly to a large number of people. Doctors may not be able to **contain** the spread of the virus. In 2019, for instance, many countries around the world had outbreaks of measles. It was one of the worst years for measles outbreaks in a long time.

FAST FACT

Scientists believe that the measles **vaccine** saved more than 23 million lives between 2000 and 2018.

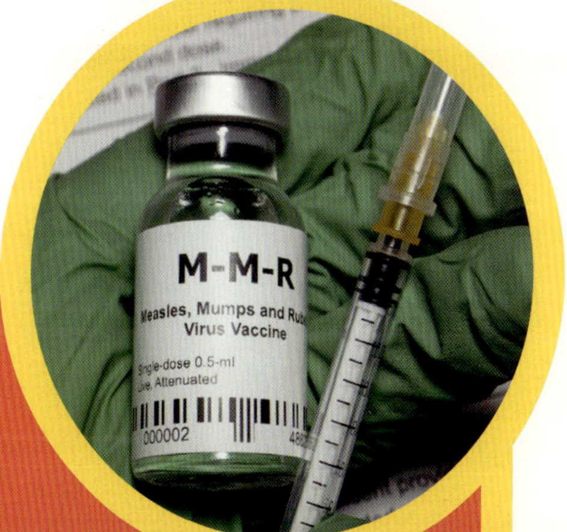

The measles virus attacks white blood cells.

What Is Measles?

Measles is a disease that is caused by the measles virus. Its symptoms include respiratory infections, rashes, and flu-like symptoms. Measles can lead to major health problems and even death.

The measles virus has been around for hundreds of years. A Persian doctor wrote about measles in the 9th century. Settlers likely brought the disease to the Americas in the 1500s. In 1912, experts began to track cases of measles in the United States. Many people born before 1960 had the disease. There were millions of cases each year. Finally, a vaccine was developed in 1963.

U.S. Measles Cases from 1954 to 2008

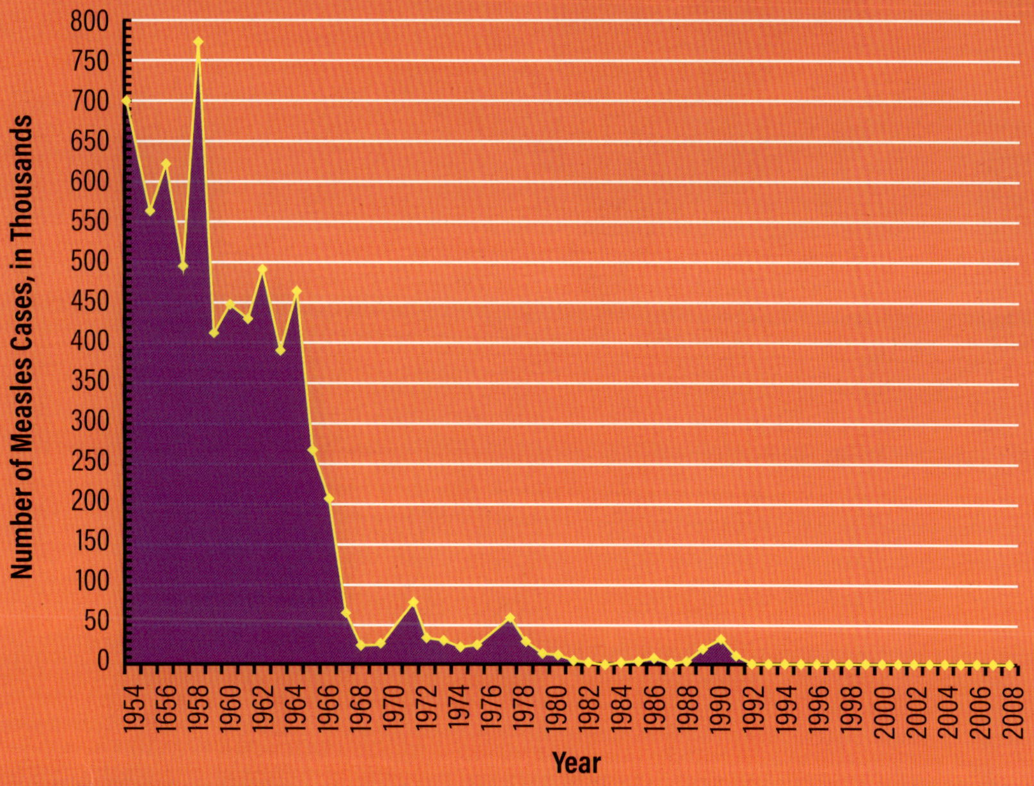

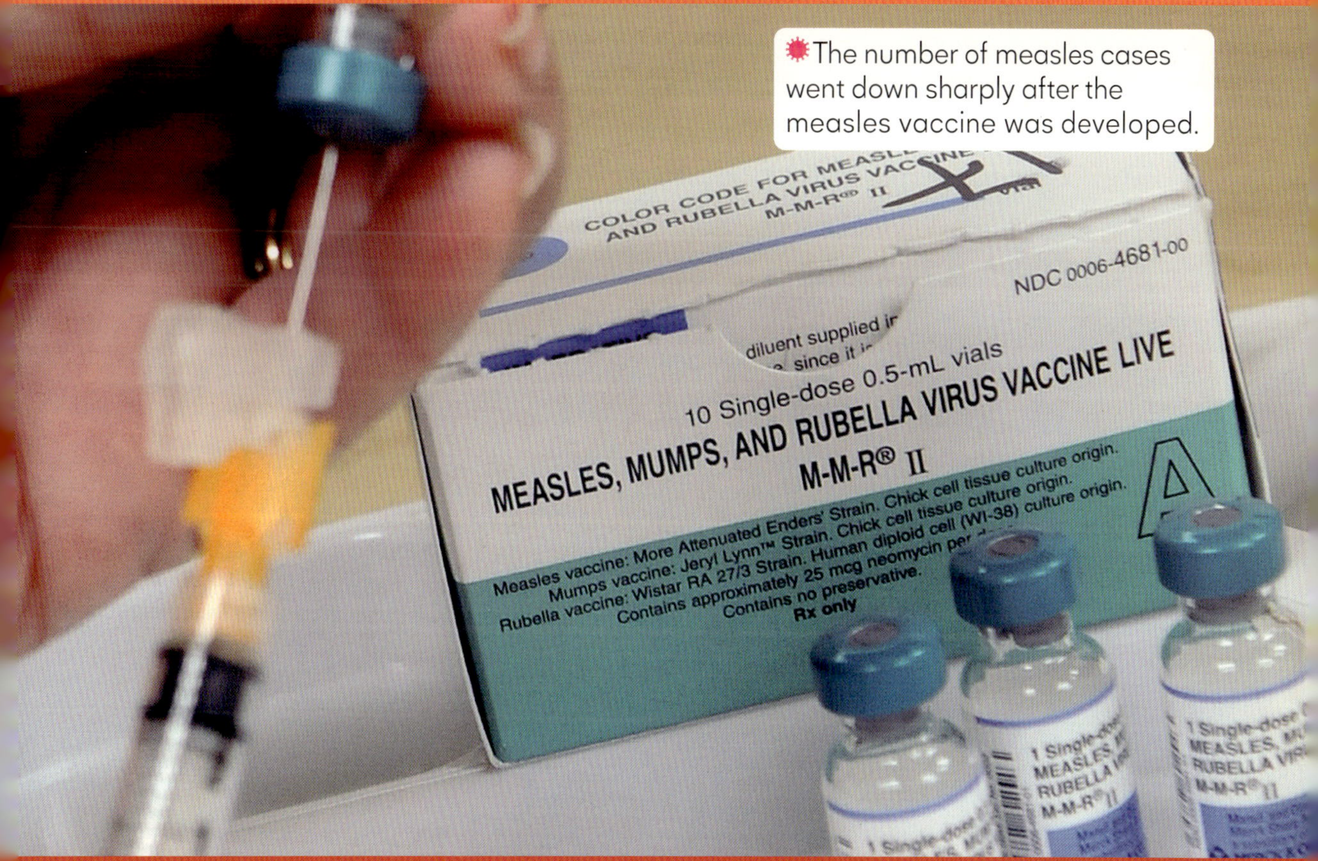

The number of measles cases went down sharply after the measles vaccine was developed.

Measles leaves many people bedridden until they recover.

Spreading the Virus

Measles is one of the most **contagious** diseases in the world. It spreads easily from person to person. The virus comes out in droplets from an infected person's nose, mouth, and throat when the person coughs, sneezes, or talks. Other people may then breathe in the droplets. Droplets land on objects, too. The measles virus can live on objects for up to two hours. People who touch the objects can get the virus if they touch their nose, mouth, or eyes without washing their hands first.

Measles is so contagious that people can get it just by being in the same room as someone who has the disease. Measles is most common in children, but adults often have worse symptoms. People who have had measles build **antibodies** to the disease. Antibodies keep most people from ever getting measles again.

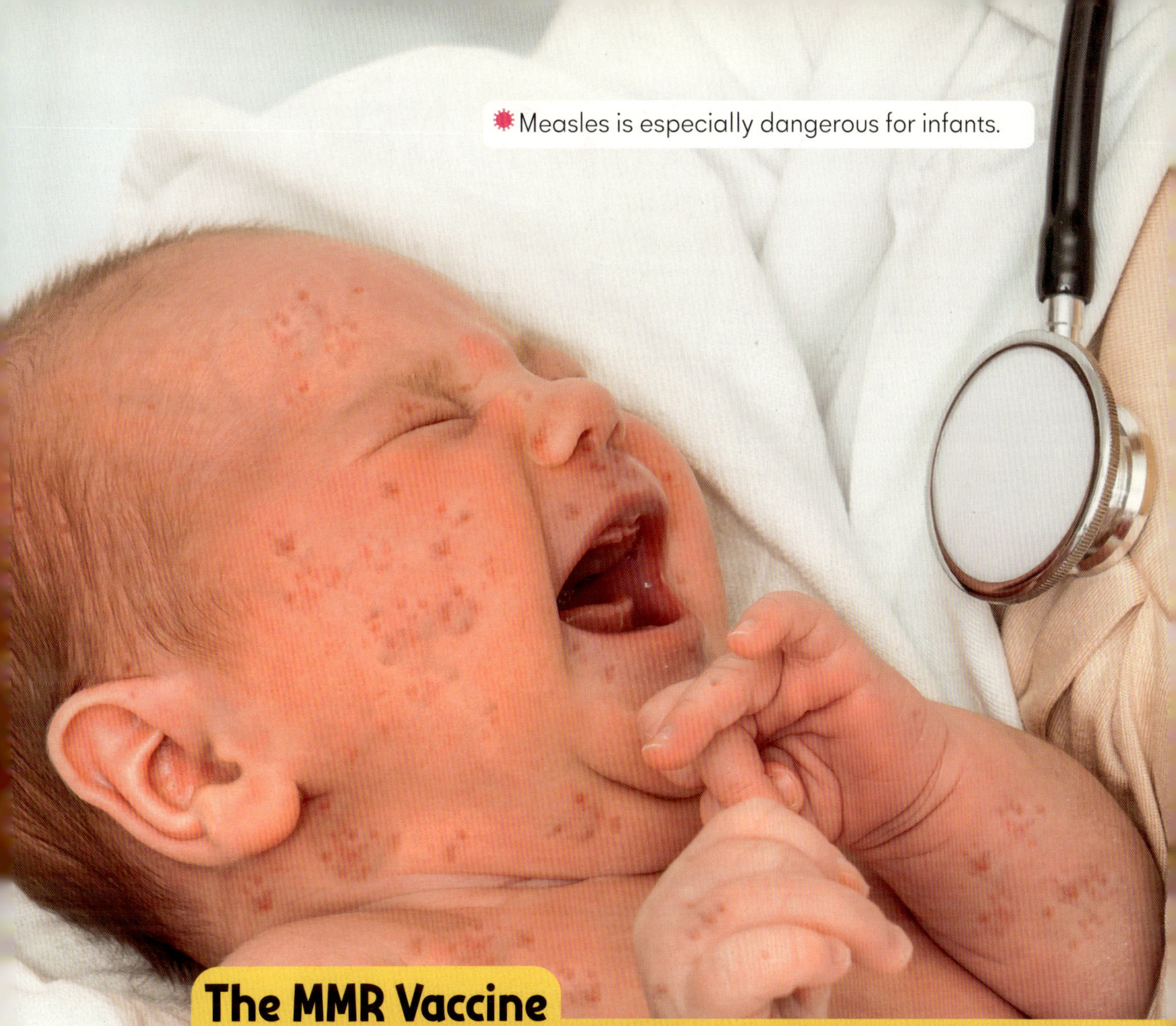

Measles is especially dangerous for infants.

The MMR Vaccine

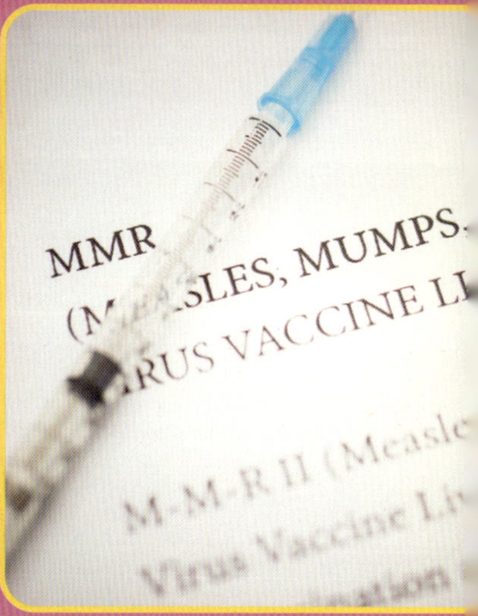

Rubella is a disease that is sometimes called German measles. It is caused by a different virus than measles. Still, the two viruses are similar in some ways. Both spread through droplets, cause a fever and rash, and only infect humans. Many people get a vaccine called the MMR vaccine that protects against measles, rubella, and another disease called mumps.

Signs, Symptoms, and Treatment

People start to show signs of measles about 8 to 10 days after they are infected. At first, measles just feels like a bad cold. People may have a fever and red eyes. A cough, runny nose, and sore throat are common, too. Tiny white spots start to form inside the mouth two to three days later. A red rash appears about three to five days after people first get sick. Most times, the rash starts on the face and neck. It then spreads to other parts of the body. The rash may be itchy. It lasts about four to seven days.

There is no cure for measles, and there are no drugs to fight the disease. Most of the time, measles goes away on its own after several days. Bed rest is the most common treatment.

Vaccines prevent young children from getting potentially deadly viruses.

Herd Immunity

Nine out of ten people who have not had the measles vaccine will get the disease if they come in contact with an infected person. **Herd immunity** helps lower this number greatly.

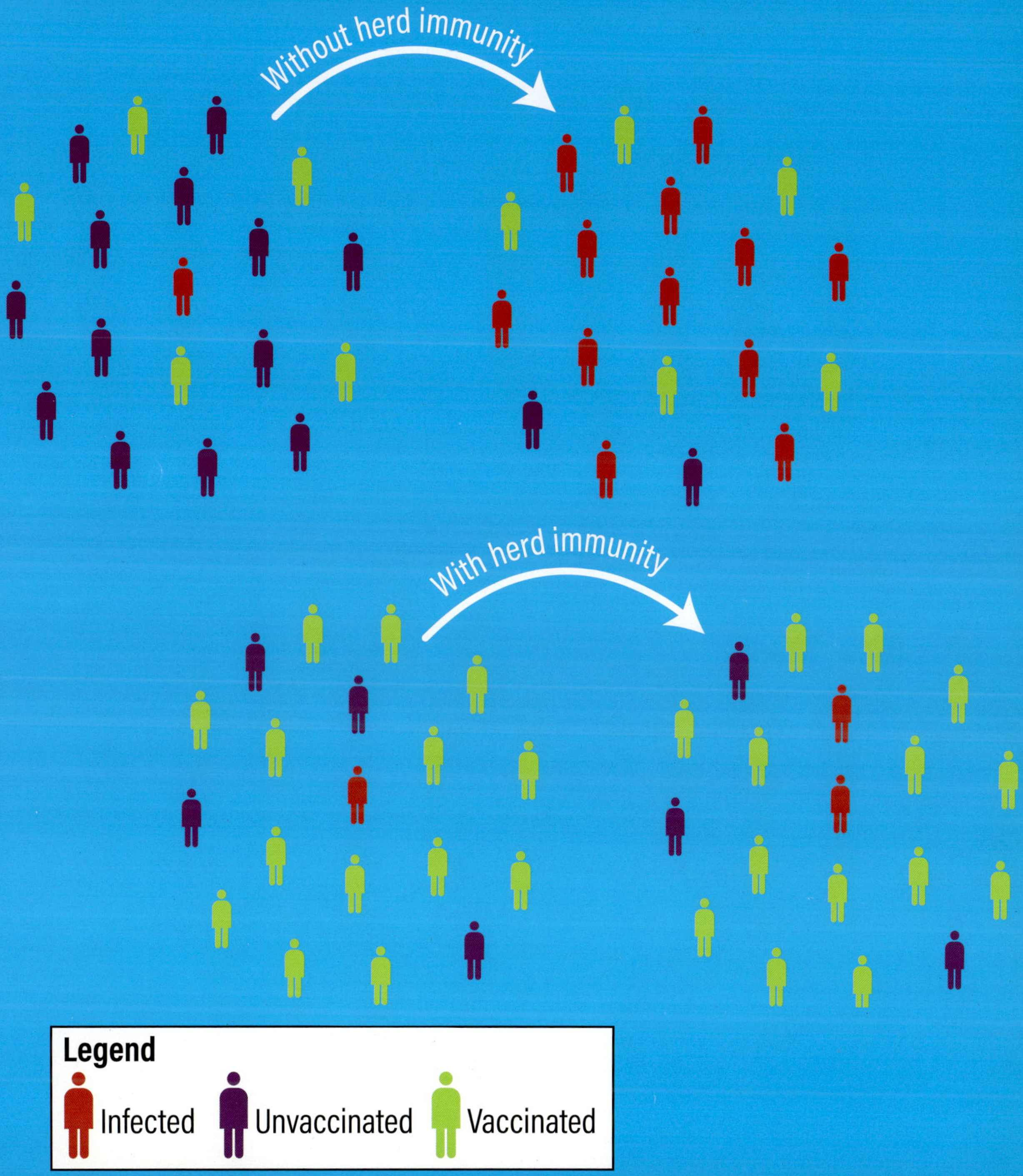

During outbreaks, press conferences are held to remind people how deadly and damaging measles can be.

Measles Outbreaks, 2019

In 2000, measles was declared eliminated from the United States. However, unvaccinated travelers kept bringing the disease back to the country. There were a few hundred cases a year, at most. That changed in 2019. There were small measles outbreaks in 31 states. About 1,300 people were infected.

Even one case of measles can lead to many more. The vaccine is the only way to protect people from the disease. Laws were put in place to help stop the spread of measles. In New York, for example, all children must now get the vaccine before they start school or daycare.

To Vaccinate or Not

Nearly 75 percent of U.S. measles cases in 2019 were due to outbreaks in New York. The outbreaks mainly took place in communities where people chose not to have their children vaccinated. For some, vaccination goes against their beliefs. Others think vaccines are harmful or unsafe. The measles vaccine is very safe. It has been used for about 60 years.

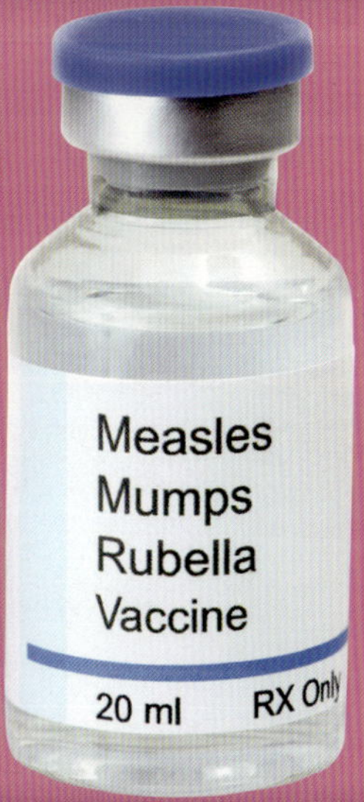

Global View

Measles cases began to rise in the mid-2010s. Not enough people were getting the vaccine. There were 30 percent more cases in 2017 than in 2016. That number grew even higher in 2018. There were more than twice as many cases as there were in 2017. About 140,000 people died of measles in 2018. Most were under the age of five.

By 2019, there were measles outbreaks all over the world. There were over 500,000 cases in more than 180 countries. Many of the outbreaks took place in countries where a large number of people had not received the vaccine. Some countries where most people are vaccinated had outbreaks in 2019, too.

Some places put up signs and enact preventative measures to help stop measles outbreaks.

Mapping the 2019 Measles Outbreak from January to June

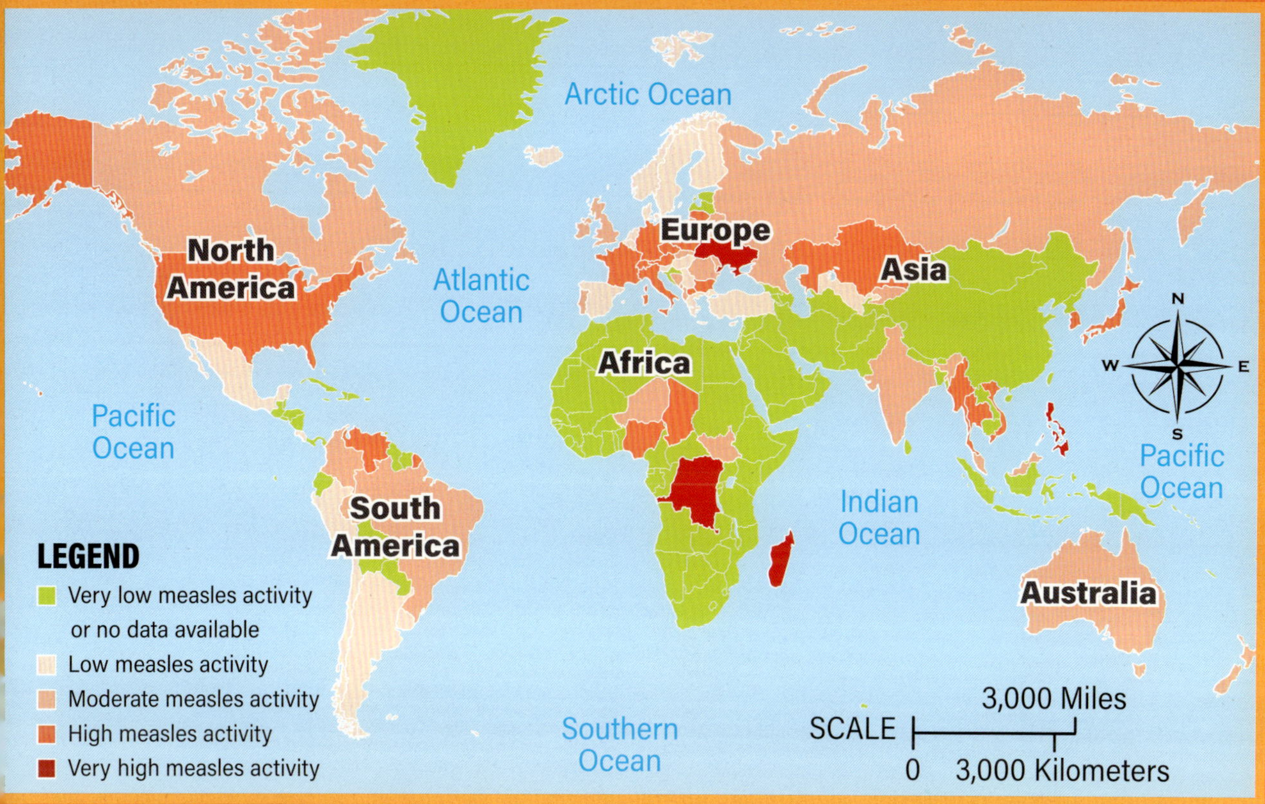

In the **first three months of 2018**, 163 countries reported **28,124 measles cases**.

In the **first three months of 2019**, 170 countries reported **112,163 measles cases**.

The Americas saw a **60 percent increase** in measles cases between **2018** and **2019**.

Science and Research

In 1954, a scientist named John Enders and a doctor named Thomas C. Peebles wanted to learn more about measles. They took a sample of the measles virus from the blood and throat swab of an 11-year-old boy. Then, they used it to make a vaccine. After their vaccine was approved for use in 1963, measles cases started to go down.

A second vaccine came out in 1968. It was made by Maurice Hilleman. This vaccine gave better protection from measles. It is the only measles vaccine in use in the United States today. Children get two doses of the vaccine. They get the first dose when they are about a year old, and they get the second dose between the ages of four and six.

FAST FACT

About 95 percent of people need to get vaccinated to stop the spread of measles. However, the number of children who get the vaccine has gone down in recent years. Worldwide, only about 86 percent of children received the first dose of the measles vaccine in 2019. Less than 70 percent received the second dose. This means that people are not fully protected, outbreaks will still happen, and more people will die.

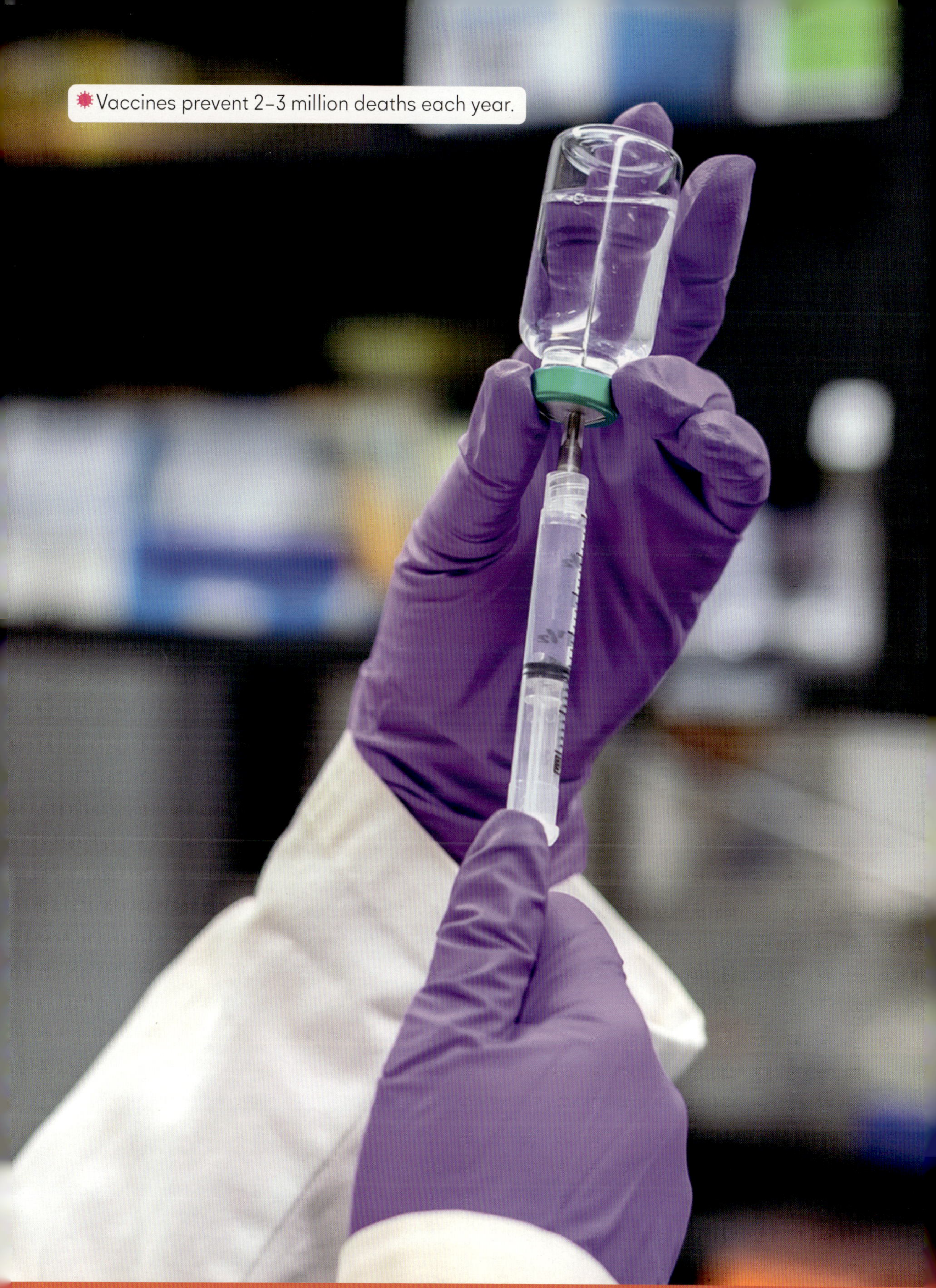

Vaccines prevent 2–3 million deaths each year.

Becoming more educated about preventable viruses and getting vaccinated helps to stop these viruses from spreading.

Measles Today

By 2020, the measles outbreak in the United States seemed to be under control. However, measles is still a problem in many parts of the world. Measles outbreaks are most common in developing countries. Healthcare systems are often not as good in these parts of the world. Not everyone can get vaccinated. Many people live in crowded areas. Children may not be healthy. The virus spreads quickly. More people get sick.

Sometimes, people do not know why they need vaccines or how vaccines help. As a result, they do not get vaccinated. Others think vaccines do more harm than good. In certain places, **civil unrest** keeps people from getting to clinics. People who live in rural areas are sometimes hard to reach. Health experts watch for measles outbreaks. The sooner they spot new cases, the faster they can stop the spread.

How Contagious Is Measles?

The average number of people that a sick person infects depends on how contagious a virus is. The measles virus is one of the most contagious viruses in the world. On average, one infected person spreads the measles virus to 12–18 others.

Comparing Viruses

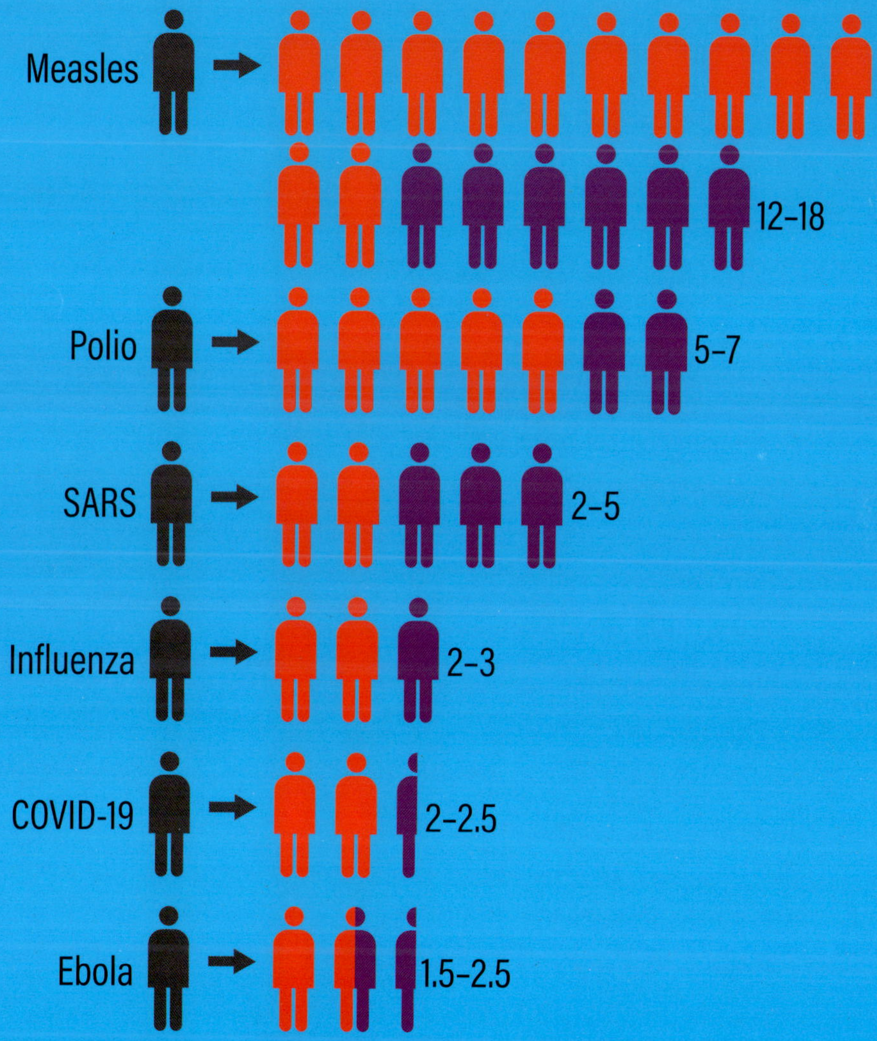

Measles Timeline

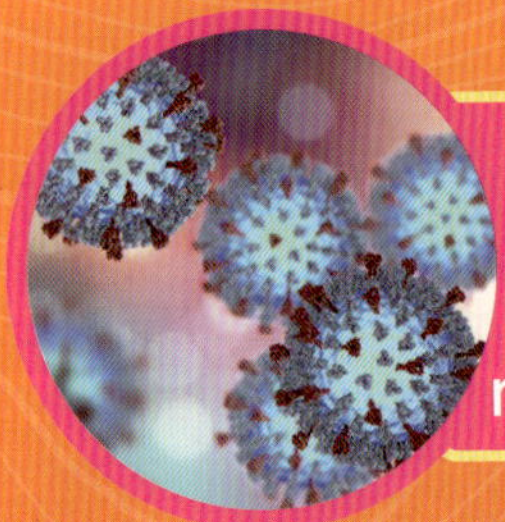

1912
Scientists begin tracking all measles cases in the United States.

1916
Measles kills nearly 12,000 people in the United States.

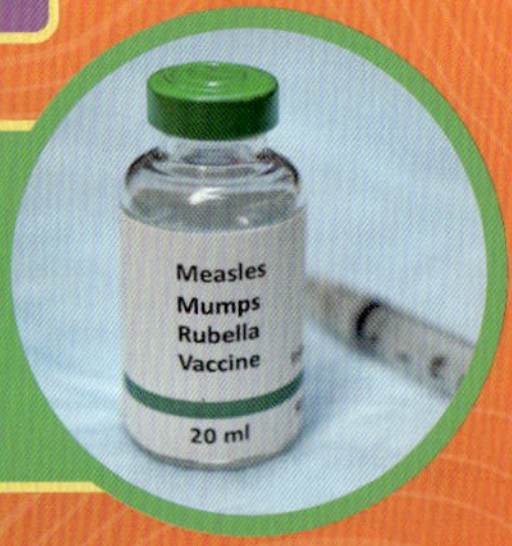

1963
The first measles vaccine is approved for use.

1968
A second measles vaccine is released.

1981
There is a huge drop in the number of measles cases in the United States.

2019
The biggest outbreak of measles since 2006 occurs worldwide. There are 1,282 cases in the United States.

2020
During the first half of the year, only 12 new cases of measles are reported in the United States.

ACTIVITY
Spreading a Virus

People come in contact with viruses every day. Viruses are all around us. They can get inside the body and attack. Some viruses spread quickly. Measles is one of them. Try this activity to see how easy it is for measles to spread from one person to the next.

What You Need

- White paper
- Tape
- Scissors
- Crayons or colored pencils

What to Do

1. Draw pictures of tiny viruses on the white paper. Make viruses of all shapes, sizes, and colors.
2. Next, cut out the viruses. You should now have a pile of virus cutouts.
3. Use tape to stick a virus to any object you touch. Pretend each of these objects is now covered with the virus. Do this for 30 minutes.
4. Look around the room. How many objects did you touch? Are there more than you thought? Anyone who touches these objects and then touches their nose, mouth, or eyes could get infected with the virus, too.

MEASLES QUIZ

1
Which diseases does the MMR vaccine protect against?

2
How many people died of measles in 2018?

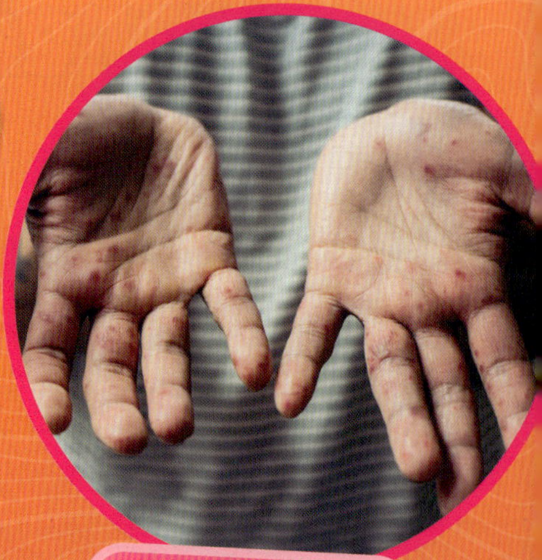

4
How does measles spread?

3
When was the first measles vaccine released?

5
Is rash a symptom of measles?

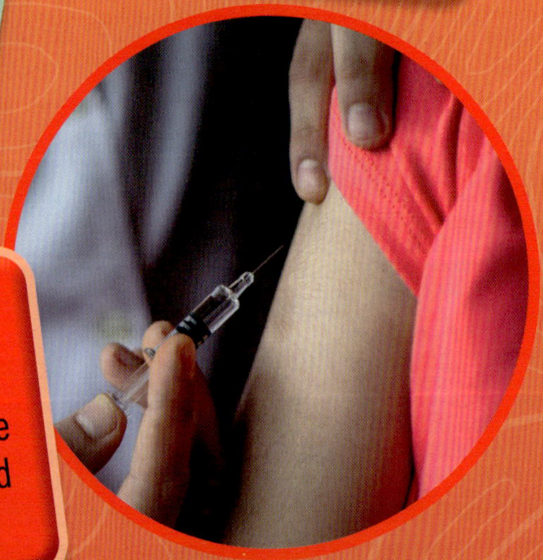

6
How can people stop the spread of measles?

7
How many U.S. states had measles outbreaks in 2019?

8
On average, how many people does one person with measles infect?

ANSWERS
1. Measles, mumps, and rubella
2. About 140,000
3. 1963
4. Contact with droplets from an infected person or contaminated objects
5. Yes
6. By getting vaccinated
7. 31
8. 12–18

Key Words

antibodies: substances made in special cells of the body to help fight off infection
civil unrest: fighting between different people or groups within the same part of the world
contagious: moves easily from one person to another
contain: keep under control
diseases: illnesses that have certain signs and symptoms
herd immunity: the resistance to the spread of a disease within a population that occurs when a high percentage of the population is vaccinated against that disease
infect: contaminate a person or object with a disease-causing germ
vaccine: a substance made from a small amount of a disease-causing germ to help provide immunity against that germ
viruses: very small germs that get inside the body and spread

Index

Published by AV2
14 Penn Plaza, 9th Floor
New York, NY 10122
Website: www.av2books.com

Library of Congress Control Number: 2020943903

ISBN 978-1-7911-3226-2 (hardcover)
ISBN 978-1-7911-3227-9 (softcover)
ISBN 978-1-7911-3228-6 (multi-user eBook)
ISBN 978-1-7911-3229-3 (single-user eBook)

Printed in Guangzhou, China
1 2 3 4 5 6 7 8 9 0 24 23 22 21 20

082020
101119

Art Director: Terry Paulhus Project Coordinator: Priyanka Das

Every reasonable effort has been made to trace ownership and to obtain permission to reprint copyright material. The publisher would be pleased to have any errors or omissions brought to its attention so that they may be corrected in subsequent printings.

The publisher acknowledges Getty Images, iStock, and Shutterstock as its primary image suppliers for this title.